FROST CHILD

JAY G DAVIS

Dedicated to the Little Girl

that lives inside all of us.

ACKNOWLEDGEMENTS

What a journey this has been for me. When I first started writing Frost Child it barely had a name. It was just a dream and oftentimes I could not see a clear path to this being a reality.

But **God**!

I would like to acknowledge **my daughter,** for being my frost baby and giving me the reason to live my life and to make it better.

I want to thank all my **"Mothers,"** that contributed to my examples of what a mother should be.

I am thankful for my **sister,** who allowed me to share a part of her story unselfishly.

Thanks to **Terry Pate,** who started the journey of editing Frost Child for me and did an amazing job.

I would like to thank all my **spiritual guides,** that allowed

God to use them to show me love and guidance.

To my amazing Publisher, **OGW Publishing,** you came at

the right time to bring this to fruition.

Finally to all the unmentionables thank you.

The journey was hard but necessary

Volume 1

THE SET UP

"Ariel!"

"Yes, ma'am".

"Stop looking out that window and get ready for church," said Mrs. Hallstead. Mrs. Hallstead was my new foster momma.

Another day of Sunday service, but at least that gets me out of this house. The only time we leave the house is for church or school. We don't have activities we are involved in and I don't really know any of the neighborhood kids. So I guess you can say I live in a bubble. A bubble I created to protect me from anything that was called reality.

At five years old, I should not be worrying about what is going to happen if my big sister doesn't start talking soon. I am still still trying to adjust to being in a foster home. I have no clue what a foster home is. It's 1975 and life don't look so promising to me. Who the hell is my Momma? What's her name? Where did she go, and is her ass coming back?

Adjust... I keep hearing that word in my mind. That's what the social worker kept saying when they picked us up from Big Momma's house almost six months ago. But my mind is still trying to figure out, how do you adjust to a decision you had no say so in? The foster home looks like a new world but if I had gone down the street and turned right, in about fifteen no more than twenty minutes, I would have been right back where I started...Swanson Home.

Yep! It sounded like a housing project courtesy of the federal government because it was (as Black folk referred to it) "The Projects." The projects was made up of mostly single Black women households with one or more kids, and if they were lucky, a man came around every so often to either take them to the grocery store or get them pregnant again. Well that's what Big Momma used to say. Either way, where we ended up we could have jogged back to our beginning. I guess Big Momma was just too tired of taking care of my sister and I. So she turned her back and acted like she didn't see the Aries K car that pulled up almost six months ago. Let me take you to where my journey began.

YOU GOT A FAMILY

Why are we sitting here in our best clothes that we own? Why are the rest of my things in a plastic bag beside me? Why does it feel like my life is about to change forever?

"Ariel."

"Yes, Big Momma".

"I want you and your sister Delilah to remember you got a family, you understand me?"

"Yes ma'am," I replied. But really I wanted to say, "No, I have no clue what you are talking about," but if you were raised in the 70's, you knew no form of disrespect was tolerated by a child.

"I did the best I could for you and Delilah, but I'm tired and I have to let 'em come and take you. Someone done told the people on me."

I'm thinking, "What people and go where?" It must be somewhere nice because I have my best dress on so I plan on having a good time.

"Baby, I want you to remember we love you and you got a family."

I responded to Big Momma by giving her a hug and she gave me one of her juicy kisses. Yuck! She always smells like mothballs.

"Delilah baby, do you hear what Big Momma said? You got a family!"

"Yes, ma'am," she responded in her quiet-toned voice. She's only six and shy. I do most of the talking for the both of us. A car pulls up and Big Momma starts for the door in her 6'4" frame (she drags her left leg and always has a juicy mouth). She looked tired and worn out like most of the Black women I knew. I didn't realize it at the time but my views are being set for me at an early age of the "Angry Black Woman."

A white woman and a Black woman entered the house in blue suits. They looked at Delilah and me as if we knew what was going on.

The white woman spoke to Big Momma like she had a conversation with her before.

"Ms. Freeman."

"Yes, Mizz Porter", Big Momma replied.

"Have you told the girls what is taking place today?"

"I told them they got a family!" she said in a very stern voice.

Ms. Porter didn't seem to know how to respond to that comment so she turned to my sister and me and began speaking.

"Okay girls. My name is Ms. Porter and this is Ms. Johnson. We are here today to remove you from this residence and take you to your new home."

At five years old, I didn't know what a residence was and if it was anything new. "I'll take it but can my Big Momma come?"

She continued to say things such as it's going to change us and we will have to adjust. They told us that they will be there to help us with the new changes that are about to take place. Tears began to roll down my face. I knew at that moment that things had just hit the fan. Even at five years old, I knew that sadness was going to play a major role in my life for a long time.

Ms. Johnson began to speak, "Okay girls. Hug your momma and tell her good-bye." We did just that...no questions asked. When you don't know you have rights, you don't use them. Things are getting pretty intense, Big Momma begins to cry and scream, "You got a family!" and she keeps repeating it until it's ringing in my ear. By now it was obvious that the social workers were getting uneasy, especially Mizz Porter.

People can become intimidated when a Black woman raises her voice.

We're being pushed towards the door by the two ladies. I am looking back at my surroundings trying to make a mental note of what it looks like so I can find my way back, but Big Momma's big 6'4" frame is blocking my view. She's dragging that heavy leg pretty good, screaming at the top of her lungs, "YOU GOT A FAMILY!" We finally got to the car and you know it wouldn't be the projects if we didn't have a crowd waiting outside to see what all the ruckus was about. Some folks are seen shaking their heads and some are saying, "It's a damn shame what they are doing to them kids." I began to scream, "I don't want to go! I don't care how new it is. I will take this run down, no water running project home as long as Delilah and Big Momma are in it!" When the social worker began to put us in the car, I looked at Delilah through my tears and she was emotionless. No tears, no screaming. Nothing! I try to be like her and stop crying but my heart won't stop hurting. I feel like if I leave, Big Momma won't be happy anymore. I was already making myself responsible for other people's emotions even at five. I was creating my beginning stages of people pleasing, trying to find something to hold onto that wouldn't let go of me.

We are finally in the back seat with our plastic bags between us, when the door shuts and the car is facing toward the road. I turned around to see Mizz Porter go up to Big Momma, as she's being comforted by a neighbor. She hands Big Momma an envelope and for some reason, that just calms her down. Meanwhile I'm still wondering how to make my escape later when we get to the new place and how to get mute Delilah to come back with me. I look at Big Momma and she looks defeated, tired and ashamed all at once. Ms. Johnson is in the front seat, basically doing nothing but being a presence. Hmmph. Basically being a token so it won't look so bad to the neighborhood. Society had already started its manipulation of the minds of two little Black girls and introduced us to "the Black Token Presence".

Mizz Porter gets in the car and starts the engine. I began to realize a plan b is going to have to be my way out. I ride away looking backwards, not realizing I would spend the next eighteen years of my life looking backwards.

THE NEW PLACE

The drive to the new place seems like forever; the only excitement was the stop to McDonalds. I look at Delilah and try to communicate with her without moving my lips but she is clearly in another dimension of her own. I'm still preparing for the great escape but as we near this red brick house I begin to think maybe it won't be so bad. It even has a car outside of the house, which means I may be able to get to McDonalds more often than when I lived with Big Momma. Big Momma didn't have a car and if you saw a car in the projects, it was either a cab or somebody's boyfriend dropping them off.

We pull up at the house and a lady comes out looking excited to see us. What stood out the most about her was her left arm was missing. She had on a long sleeve shirt but it was empty on the left side. I made a mental note to ask her if she was going to get an arm like the Bionic Woman had. Everything else about her seemed normal. She had legs and teeth, and she had the roundest face I had ever seen. Big Momma's face was long like her body.

As we neared the door to the house, even at five my instincts told me that this was an interview and if I wanted to be able to stay at this house with the red bricks and car in front of it, I better get into character. So I smiled as big as I could for the both of us. Delilah was still sitting in the car refusing to move.

I guess it was Ms. Johnson's turn to be the lead social worker because she began to speak to the lady with one arm, while Mizz Porter sat in the car with Delilah.

"Hello, Mrs. Hallstead! These are the girls. Ariel is five and Delilah is six."

"They are prettier in person," exclaimed Mrs. Hallstead. Now I was dark but I had what you call "pretty hair" and Della was light skinned or red bone, a term used often in the Black community when referring to a fair skinned Black person. Her hair was soft and wavy. So according to the standards of beauty in the Black community, she had it going on. I just had pretty hair. Mrs. Hallstead was dark so I guess she didn't mind that I was either.

I begin to wonder what I'm supposed to call this lady with one arm. Momma? That sounds normal in my head but I don't really know anyone but Big Momma and we always said "Big" before Momma. I really don't know anything about my real Momma so I had no blueprint of a mother- daughter relationship.

Mrs. Hallstead didn't seem like a Big Momma type and she didn't smell like mothballs or have a juicy mouth, so at that moment I decided Momma it is!

"Hello, Ariel," said Mrs. Hallstead. I looked at her and put on my 1000 watt smile I had been practicing in my mind, not even realizing that would become my mask for many years to come.

"Hello, Ma'am", I said. "You want to be my momma?" Yeah I went straight for the kill. If this is going to be my new home, I need to secure it before some other kids show up. Mrs. Hallstead chuckled and said, "I would like that very much."

I replied, "Since you're gonna be my momma, can I call you Momma?"

She said, "If you would like to."

I thought this was easy. I got a new place to stay and I got to call someone Momma. Now all I have to do is convince Delilah to do the same. And just like that I had a new momma. This was the beginning of a series of "Mommas" for me. I was learning early you can attach yourself to women and they could become your Momma even if your own Momma didn't want you. You just have to keep the mask on with the 1000 watt smile and be nice to them. I was learning early to put the mask on and pretend this was my reality.

Finally Delilah decided to get out of the car because the social workers had to leave. Mrs. Hallstead waved at them as they pulled off and I waved too. I figured if she was my momma, I should do what she does. Delilah just stood in a trance. What I didn't know was my sister was displaying exactly what I was feeling...trauma. I would discover later in life that her ability to feel, deal and heal early allowed her to save her mental state... not me. I pushed it aside and became the ultimate people pleaser.

"Okay girls. Let's get you settled in your bedroom." Bedroom? What is that? At Big Mommas house we slept on some mattresses in a room or in the living room. Mrs. Hallstead was still speaking about dressers and drawers to put our clothes in. I was thinking this must be the life. They even have designated areas for your clothes too! I'm used to finding everything we owned in Big Momma's room. I'm looking at Delilah like, "Don't mess this up for me. Speak!"

She didn't and wouldn't for almost six months. She was a brilliance that had lost her voice at the tender age of six.

Volume 4

BIG MOMMA

Big Momma looked at the Aries K car drive out the projects that were taking her hearts with her.

"I know," said Ms. Laney as she looked at Big Momma with pity. She was an older lady that lived in the same projects but a few streets over. Her daughter and Greta were good friends. That was Big Momma's hearts momma name. Her first name was Lynora but we called her by her middle name Greta. But right now Big Momma wanted to know, "Where the devil is that gal at? All them gals wanna do is run 'dem streets" she said, still shaking her head.

"Chasing men and getting drunk all the time. They act like they don't know the Lawd. Lawdy!" exclaimed Big Momma. "I knows Crip is turning over in his grave. I am just tired Laney! I am tired."

Big Momma was allowing herself to feel the pain of losing the girls, if just for a moment. Big Momma was always practicing her good Christian values and never thought that she needed time for her own emotions. Christianity in the Black household came as both a blessing and curse. On one hand you were sold out for Christ and on the other hand you couldn't see the pain in your own life because you were too busy practicing a belief that you didn't quite know the true meaning of. Instead, you inherited the generational practices from your ancestors and were never taught how to manifest light and love in your life because it was supposed to be non-existent for descendants of slaves. Nowhere in the world is the Black woman allowed to feel her true pain so Big Momma did what she was taught to do by many women before her... suppress her feelings and pray that Gawd would make a way.

"I knows you are, Connie", said Ms. Laney. Connie was Big Momma's first name. "You did all you could, suga".

Laney's daughter Candice was also known as Cupcake. She was just as wild as Greta. We called her Cupcake because all she ate when she was a little girl was chocolate cupcakes. But these gals not little no mo and they ain't nothing but trouble.

"Dem gals of ours are just too fast for their own britches!" Laney pats Big Momma on the back and leaves to head home. Big Momma goes into the house dragging her leg as the crowd disperses in the neighborhood.

Big Momma looks in her bedroom to find her husband Clarence (or Poppa, as her hearts used to call him) with a bottle in his hand.

All he does is drink and sleep she thought. I am a Christian woman and he doesn't respect Gawd at all. He thinks I don't know where he is when he gets up at night but I ask Gawd every morning to take this away from me. "Why didn't Gawd take him and not my hearts?" Her eyes misted over but just for a second. She heads to the table and grabs the envelope out her big bible that Mizz Porter had given her earlier. Enclosed was the name and address of the foster family where her hearts were going.

She closes her eyes, feeling the pain of defeat she allowed herself to feel. The tears started like running water through a faucet and she just could not seem to turn it off..

The anthem of the Black Woman: pain... trauma... heartache...repeat.

"Gawd you took my brother, now you done took my hearts," Big Momma said aloud in her defeated voice one last time.

"I ain't got nothing left."

And as quickly as she allowed herself to feel, she knew she had to adjust too, just like that white social worker lady was telling the girls. So she stopped, wiped her eyes and thought,

"Where is that gal at!?" And just like that her mask was readjusted over her face.

My house needs to be cleaned from top to bottom, she thought, And she needs to get her behind here because her sister Wanda Faye is nowhere to be found. I don't know how their Momma was raising them gals because they are as fast as they can be. Greta got my house filled up with all these babies and it's only a matter of time before her sister will have some boy all up her skirt.

Shaking her head she looked out the screen door and headed for her kitchen, dragging her leg and wiping her juicy mouth. "Lawd! They daddy turning over in his grave."

WANDA FAYE

The projects were good for housing the kids and the women but never allowed the men to live in the house, which made absolutely no sense. Let's just say "the system" invented the broken Black households.

Now Greta's sister, Wanda Faye, was a cute 'lil chocolate project girl. She was fifteen years old with wavy black hair hanging down her back and although she wasn't a "red bone", she had many admirers in the neighborhood. Sometimes, I swear the men act like they are in cages, and the women are pieces of meat that they are waiting to be thrown to them just so they can devour it and pass it out like waste, and any young thing would satisfy that appetite.

As Wanda Faye walked she began to reflect:

"This life is not what I signed up for. When my momma was alive, we had a house and a Daddy but when momma died things got out of control. My Daddy started drinking all the time and he was not able to raise us after my momma died. So he moved to Virginia and brought us with him, to be close to his side of the family, the Daniel's. I am the middle child of Juanita and James, Greta is the oldest girl at sixteen and Shelia is the baby girl (she'thirteen). Lil James was the only boy they brought to Virginia; he was 9 months older than me. Although my momma died when I was only five (it still seems like only yesterday), it's been ten years. Sheila used to stay with us but when my Daddy died, my Aunt Anna (my Daddy's youngest sister) came and got Shelia and took her to live in New York with her and her daughter Annie. When Daddy died, the Daniels family began picking over us like we were a dog litter. We were divided by color and ages. Hmph...the Daniel family version of the slave auction block.

I didn't want to come to Big Momma's house when my momma died but since Daddy was still living, he wanted his oldest sister to help him raise us. I bet my Daddy turned over in his grave, like Big Momma always says when we do something wrong. I wonder if he turns over when Poppa gets on the mattress with Greta.

Now when my momma was alive, she did not take no mess off of my Daddy. He came home every night from wherever he was. I used to hear my granddaddy say (when we lived in North Carolina) that my Daddy was trifling and "He ain't got a pot to piss in and a window to throw it out," but every time he came home, he had a pocket full of money. My momma had a pot full of food that she would sit in the window until it cooled off before we would eat dinner. Sometimes I wanted to tell my granddaddy to come by the house so he could see the pot sitting in the window full of food but nobody ever listened to kids. So I just made sure my Daddy never pissed in the pot.

My daddy was the best daddy a girl could have. We lived in North Carolina because my momma's family (the Wesley's) was from there and she wanted to be close to her family. I used to hear my uncles tell my momma," Crip is a piece of shit for a man!" That was my Daddy nickname ...his real name was James.

Then they would say, "He don't mean you no good, Juanita," (That was my momma name) but I guess my momma felt otherwise because from what I can remember, my Daddy was always grabbing my momma's big booty and they always seem to have fun, 'specially when they had cups in their hands.

When my momma was alive we had clothes for days. They were clean and pressed and we always smelled like baby powder. People would stare at us because we came in all shades of black from light skin, hazelnut to mocha. All of us had what Black folks call "pretty hair" since it was wavy and hanging down our backs in a long ponytail just like our momma. When we walked down the street people would say "there goes Juanita and her pretty kids." My daddy used to stick out his chest because he thought all the men were looking at my momma and her kids. I would catch the men looking at my momma booty. It was big. When nobody was watching I would stick my booty out and try to walk like my momma. Sometimes she would catch me and give me that eye roll and suck her teeth. I would run and hide behind my daddy legs, laughing hysterically. Those were happier times. Then one day my momma and daddy took a trip to New York, taking my sister Shelia with them. I never saw my momma again. I heard all kinds of stories but I don't even remember seeing her in the casket. They said we were too little to see her like that so all the memories I have of my momma is in my head. And when I hear Big Momma say stuff about her (I don't think Big Momma liked momma 'cause all she says when she mad at us is "Ya'll act just like your crazy Momma," 'specially when she is not looking. I'd roll my eyes and suck my teeth just like my momma used to do.

Big Momma took me, my brother Lil' James and Greta, and moved us in with her and her husband, who we called Poppa. I didn't like him' cause I always catch him looking at Greta like she was a grown lady. Hmmph...nobody looked at me.

So needless to say, when my Daddy died I had to grow up real fast because Greta stopped talking and Shelia became a hellcat. Lil' James just sat and stared out the window all the time (I always wondered what he was looking at and who he was talking to). All Shelia did was fight, beat up people, take what she wanted and disrespect anybody that she didn't like, which was all of the Daniel family. They treated us differently. Some looked like they felt sorry for us while others looked like they hated us. I didn't know that the Black family had been taught to love what treats them bad and hate what comes from them; and the Daniel side of the family were the ambassadors of that curse. When they kids came over, Big Momma would show off by treating us mean. I never understood why she thought that was love. After she'd yell and scream at us for no reason, then she would make us perform for the adults. I could dance and Greta could sing so when the family came over, Big Momma would make us stand in the middle of the floor and perform over a series of songs. Lil' James didn't have to do it because he was a boy. So he got to stand around like the other kids watching me and Greta. It was the only time Big Momma seemed proud of us and as sick as it was, I craved for any attention. Maybe that's why they sent Sheila to live with Aunt Anna. I heard Aunt Anna was mean and I guess they thought she was the only one that could control my sister.

I only saw my Aunt Anna twice; at my Daddy funeral and when she came back to get Shelia six months after my Daddy died. Lil' James ran away by the time he was twelve. I overheard Big Momma say he found his way back to North Carolina and was living with my Momma side of the family or anybody that would take him in. It's been ten years now and every day I wake up hoping I can get back to North Carolina too, but that will have to wait because I can't leave Greta. This girl done went out and made two babies! Now, her girls, Delilah and Ariel! They are my heartbeats.

Ariel is my favorite because at five, she got a mouth on her. She kinda reminds me of myself when I was her age. She got that pretty brown mocha smooth skin and that long wavy hair like mine, hanging down her back. Now Delilah is a lot lighter like her real momma, Greta, and looks a lot like my mother, her grandmother Juanita. Her hair is soft and wavy but not as long as Ariel's. So I know they don't have the same daddies, but Greta is just as mute about that as she was about being pregnant.

One day she just started having stomach pains and when she came back from the hospital she had Delilah with her. I asked Big Momma where that baby came from. She just said, "Stay out of grown folks business and you bet not go out here and get one." It was really confusing so I asked Greta where the baby came from. She said the baby came out her butt. I said, "How does it get in there?" She said she didn't know. So I stopped drinking out of any cups Greta used because I didn't want no baby coming out my butt.

Eleven months later she had another baby and named her Ariel but this time she said she let this man stick something in her and it gave her a baby. I said, "What was it?" She said it was his "thing" I said, "What is a thing?" Before she could answer, Big Momma was coming into the room where the mattresses were and she told her to cut all that nasty talk out. So we never talked about how the babies got here; but I stayed on the lookout for any man referring to anything he had as a "thing." I didn't want the thing near me.

Greta stays gone most of the time so Big Momma relies on me for everything but I don't mind because I fell in love with those babies. It must be love because they make me feel warm and I want to keep them safe. I never feel that way around Big Momma unless I'm dancing. Sometimes I feel like Ariel and Delilah belong to me but I don't blame Greta for staying away from the house. I think she got tired of Poppa getting on the mattress with her. He never bothered me. He would call me Lil' Blackey and tell me to go outside and play.

I was scared of him and felt sorry for my sister. I think that's why I didn't mind watching Ariel and Delilah. I made sure he was never left alone with them.

When Greta started hanging with Cupcake, a girl in the projects, that's when she started drinking and getting high. I guess you could say she found something to numb her from having to deal with Poppa. Me and Big Momma became the Juanita and James to Delilah and Ariel.

I finally had a chance to get away for two weeks with my English teacher, who thinks I am pretty smart. She says I have potential (whatever that is) but I can never get to school on time. So, she got permission from Big Momma and I went to stay at Mrs. Hinton's house for the last two weeks of school, so I could pass. I had fun but I was missing my hood and my babies, Ariel and Delilah. As I was walking across the field, I was thinking 'bout what I was going to fix them to eat because sometimes Big Momma was too sick to fix them food. So if I didn't cook or Ms. Laney didn't bring food, they didn't eat.

As I neared Big Momma house, I heard all this screaming and I knew this argument all too well. Big Momma probably wanted Greta to clean her house and Greta was jumping out the window, leaving me to do all of it by myself but as I get closer, I hear Greta say, "Why you let them take 'em?" Take who? I'm thinking, did Poppa get arrested for getting on the mattress with Greta? I start smiling then I realize that they talking about my babies! Somebody came and got Ariel and Delilah! I took off running toward the house as fast as I could. "I can't believe you let them take my kids! Why, Big Momma, Why?" screamed Greta.

Greta reeked of alcohol. Bloodshot eyes, tears and snot covered her face.

"You've been gone for two weeks!" screamed Big Momma." I didn't know where your fast ass was so they took em!"

I just stand there frozen as I hear Big Momma scream. "I told them they got a family!"

I am thinking who is "they"? I try to figure out what's going on because, as usual, I am invisible unless it's a dish to wash or a child to watch.

I look from Big Momma to Greta and for the first time I can't utter a word. Big Momma's screaming like I have never heard her scream before. It's something in her voice that is so deep rooted and doused with pain it almost takes me to my knees. Now I am screaming "What happened? Where are they? Who took them?" but they don't even recognize that someone else has joined the screaming match.

THE SCREAMING MATCH

"I called Ms. Laney house and her gal said she hadn't seen you in four days, Greta!"

As the screaming match moves to the tiny project house, she continued to say,

"I am tired! I can't do it no mo, gal! They are gone and you just got to deal with it! Your daddy left me with you, your brother and sister, and ya'll don't listen to nothing I say! So they gone but I told them they got a family! Now stop all that crying and clean this house, gal."

What is wrong with this crazy bat, thought Greta. How she gone just let some strangers come grab my girls? Damn! I just had to get that last hit. I needed it to deal with Big Momma. I swear she hates me. But she loved my babies so why did she let the people get them? That's all I had in my life to be proud of, my babies, and she let them leave. But if Big Momma thinks I am going to stay in this house and clean, she is crazy. I gotta get this money so I can find my girls. "Lynora!" screamed Big Momma (she calls me by my first name when she mad, even though I go by my middle name). I don't look back as I climb out the window, headed to the field toward the black sedan parked in the parking lot of the projects.

I hear my sister screaming at me, "Where did you come from? You are always so quiet I didn't even notice you. Why weren't you here when they took my babies? Greta asked. You know what? Later for that. I gotta get out of here before I do something more to Big Momma than steal her money." Not today, Big Momma, maybe tomorrow but today I got to numb this pain. This is worse than Poppa coming in the room getting on that mattress.

As I neared the car, I jumped in and told the driver, "Just make me feel good" and for the next few months all I did was get high and pray to God that he took me out of my misery. The voices in my head tell me to take my life. I am too afraid to cut my wrist so I just drink and get high and hope I don't wake up. But God didn't even listen to that because when I finally allow myself to feel my reality, three months have gone by and I'm in a jail cell. Then I remember my babies and I scream in my head until it's about to explode but nobody hears me because I stopped speaking after they took my babies. Since I can't find my voice, I guess I'm still in shock. Big Momma mean ass just gave up on my girls like she did with me, my brother and sister. She couldn't have kids so when my daddy died she became a parent. My daddy was her oldest brother. They called him Crip 'cause he walked with a limp. She was a horrible substitute for a mother.

I kept trying to imagine my momma, Juanita. She was the prettiest woman I had ever seen. She had five kids and if she was alive, me and my brother and sisters would be good. I

have a sister named Wanda Faye and a brother named Lil'
James (he was named after my Daddy). Wanda Faye was
with me but they took my other sister, Sheila, to New York
to live with another Aunt. The other kid was left in North
Carolina with the Wesleys' on my momma's side of the
family. I don't think that was my daddy's kid because he
didn't show him much attention like he did Lil' James so we
left him in North Carolina after my momma's funeral. Cold
hearted bastards. And Big Momma wonders why I steal from
them. They not right. They do crazy shit and then bring God
in it. Talking about God will lead the way. Naw! All he does
is lead her nasty husband to my mattress when she pretends
like she is asleep. I don't know what's in that bible she reads
every day but some pages are missing. Now when we first got
to Big Momma's house, my daddy was still alive and he came
by every so often and saw us. He always seemed so sad,
especially when he saw me. They say I looked so much like
my momma he would just cry and hold his head but he

always had a cup. After a couple of sips out of it, it seemed to make him stop crying. I knew back at age eight that when I got old enough I would find me a cup, so I could be happy like it made my daddy. Big Momma adored my daddy. He was her oldest brother and I guess she loved the attention from him. My daddy was like a fly gangster...always coming to the house with a pocket full of money but never having a job. He treated Big Momma like gold. In his eyes she was the perfect Christian woman. Please! When he died I guess she felt like it was somehow our fault and she became the Devil. Plus I would hear the family say he died of a broken heart from my momma dying so somehow they made our existence the reason for his death. Resentment came easy from Big Momma's family; they were like a gang. If one didn't like you, none of them did.

So now all she wanted us to do was clean her damn house. But once I found out men liked my big butt and pretty hair, I was out! They introduced me to this liquid that must have been the same thing my daddy used to drink and it made me want to do all kinds of crazy stuff. I didn't care because I felt wanted and loved, and that's something that never came from Big Momma after my daddy died. And her husband thought he could feel me up and get away with it, but after I turned fourteen, I started taking his money right out his wallet. Yeah, now I had a pocket full of money (like my daddy) and no job.

Big Momma acted like she didn't know what was going on but she knew I would hear her in the room at night praying for God to take him. I never understood why she stayed with Poppa, knowing he was physically abusing me and mentally abusing her but I guess she felt the shame would be far worse than the act. But nooo, you couldn't tell Big Momma that. Sometimes, I felt like she took us in so her husband could take our innocence. Nobody protects Black girls, not even their own family. Maybe them people coming to get my kids was the best thing but ain't nobody telling me nothing. So I got to find my kids my damn self, but for now I got to find a way to get out this orange jumpsuit. Damn, I wish my momma was still here.

ARIEL AND DELILAH

I wanted to wake up from this bad dream but it's been almost three months since Delilah and I have been at the Hallsteads home. At first I thought the house with the red bricks was our path to normal, but I found that to be another lie to take to the window. You see, at five years old, the only thing that could keep me wearing the mask and not going insane was sitting at the window in our tiny bedroom. It was my direct connection to heaven. The sun shined directly through the window and it gave me endless possibilities to pray to God to return our real momma to us. I would talk to God about everything. I would pray every day to God to please send my momma for us. I didn't have a clue what she looked like but I knew that if she came, she would know her girls and we would be saved. I just needed to be saved from this bubble that had me and my sister trapped and was trying to suffocate our utter existence. Delilah had died a million times in three months and I couldn't get her to speak. She had become a mute, never uttering a word. A brilliance that would take years to be discovered, because the Devil came for her early. "Delilah! Please say something. Please," I whispered. "If you don't start talking, they're going to send you back and I don't want to be here by myself."

The more I began to understand the woman with the one arm and her husband I called daddy, the more I realized we were just there to fill a void for them. They never had children and I overheard them telling some of the church members (at one of our many functions we attended) that we were a blessing from God. Let's just say we opened and closed the church doors so much and that car I thought would be taking me to McDonalds, had Green Street Baptist etched in it like what we call a GPS today.

Now on the outside Mr. Hallstead looks like a devout Christian, singing in the choir and serving on the usher board, but we soon learned at an early age you always have to give up something to get anything and this so-called safe house was not safe at all.

"Girls," Mrs. Hallstead said, "It's time for bed."

I could see the fear in my sister's eyes so I began to pray even harder before the sun was fully set. You see when the sun was up she was safe. It was only when God went away that Delilah became a victim to Mr. Hallstead. A church going man but ain't no God in him... he was the Devil himself!

"Girls, say your prayers and get into your beds."

"Yes ma'am," I said, trying to be loud for the both of us.

I looked out the window and God had turned a hazy red. Is God mad at me? Is that why he allows such evil to come into the innocence of a six year old? I begin to pray even harder! I try to remember what other people do in church to get their prayers answered but nothing comes to mind.

"God stay and protect her! I'm not big or bright enough. I beg you every day and yet you go down to the earth and don't return until it's too late." Now I can hear Mr. Hallstead. "Noooooooo! God please, I promise I'll be good. Just keep the Devil out." I can see Delilah's eyes as big as saucers. We can't stop the Devil because the sun is gone and God has abandoned us, just like everyone else in our lives. The bed squeaks and I close my eyes until the sun comes back and I can try to persuade God to show my Momma where we are so she can come save us.

The next morning arrives and it's as if nothing happened. The sun is out, which means God is back to keep us safe. I am hopeful this will be the last time the Devil comes for Delilah. We are awakened by Mrs. Hallstead for school. Mr. Hallstead has already left the house to go to work. Not sure what he actually does but he wears a beige uniform with a star on it. Something like a police star but I have never seen a beige police uniform.They are normally in blue outfits.

When we lived in the projects the police were always around.

They were always white men and they never smiled.They

were nothing like the police on television; they always

seemed helpful but only to white people. I stayed far away

from them because I didn't want to go to jail. I heard Mrs.

Hallstead tell someone on the phone my real momma was in

jail. I guess she looked at them and they caught her. I don't

see police officers in Douglass Park so they must like these

Black people.

"Girls!" she screams! "Time to get up and get ready for

school." I had mastered the mask so once again I yelled loud

enough for the both of us, "Yes Momma!"

It's funny how momma just rolls off my tongue like I have

been knowing this lady all my life. I close my eyes and picture

my momma then I begin to daydream. I picture this brown

lady with plump cheeks and long wavy hair. A version of me,

but grown. I begin to smile because she is looking at me and smiling and just when she is about to hug me, I feel a pop on my head. "Ouch!" I scream!

I open my eyes and it's Delilah telling me with her eyes, "You better get ready before we are late." I smile at her because she is so pretty and although she doesn't speak, her eyes keep me entertained and sad at the same time.

I feel this ache in my chest when I allow myself to feel; when I look at her. The same kinda pain when I think of our momma so I try not to feel when I look at Delilah. I will ask God (when I sit in the window after school) why does my chest hurt when I look in Delilah's eyes? I feel responsible so I must find a solution but in the meantime we talk with our eyes as we get dressed for school. I know when she looks at the small closet, she wants me to look for her shoes; when she looks at the door, she is ready to leave. I want her to speak so the voices in my head will shut up and stop bossing me around. I feel like ten different people trying to keep everyone friendly. Mrs. Hallstead passes the small room (with the wooden door on the hinges, which functions as our cell and our room) and looks in. That's our cue to get out and head to school.

Delilah and I really have no school clothes. We wear the same outfits each week. A lot of the kids laugh at us and make fun of our clothes because Mrs. Hallstead likes to dress us in Sunday clothes like we are her real life doll babies. I want to wear pants like the other kids but Mrs. Hallstead says it's a sin. I wonder if wearing underwear is a sin. Since you have to put them on like pants, I guess, if nobody sees them it's okay with God. I am beginning to think God has a lot of rules but adults get to pick what they want to do; but as soon as I am grown, I am buying me a pair of pants.

Most of the neighborhood kids call us holy rollies. All we do is go to church and prayer meetings. God only answers grown folk prayers because I have been in that window every chance praying and even trying to persuade the voices in my head to pray but they seem like they hate God and only like me when I am mad at him. Can't find loyalty nowhere. Everyone wants a piece of my soul but nobody ever asks me what I want. When God gets my momma to come get us, I am going to stop being friends with these voices cause they are always arguing.

Someone screams, "Ariel!" I turn around and it's this girl named Brenda. She is from the neighborhood and in my class. I smile at her with that rehearsed 1000 watt smile because I don't want anyone to know my heart hurts most of the time. So I just pretend to be normal like everyone else.

"Hey Brenda!" I look her up and down admiring her outfit that looks like most of the kids walking to school (she has on beige pants and a cute yellow top and soft leather black shoes). Delilah and I have on ruffle white socks and patent leather black shoes with our Sunday best on. Even though we were not twins and are actually eleven months apart, we always wore the same thing. I guess it was easy to identify us as belonging together. The teachers loved the way we dressed and thought we were so well taken care of in our Sunday-go-to-meeting clothes. They thought we were being raised right because of some clothes. I sucked my teeth at the thought because I am confused most of the day and the other half I am pretending I am not. The simplest things could deceive some people.

I noticed a crowd gathering around Brenda and me so I began to refocus. I zoned back in on Brenda's face and she was asking me, "Why do you and your sister always dress up to go to school?"

Now I was little but I was quick with my thoughts, so I knew this 1000 watt smile was not going to get me out of this jam. I had to be quick with my response because my five year old attention span was about .05 seconds.

So I simply said, "My momma dresses us like this to be more respectful in school to the teachers." Then I hit her with that smile and said, "It's working because I got an A in English."

I saw her wheels turning in her head and I went in full throttle. "Oh and I think I heard Ms. Mallory say she wishes more kids dressed like us." Brenda thought about it, as I stood there thinking to myself, "Agree... please". I waited and she said, "I'm wearing a dress tomorrow!" A lot of the other girls started shaking their heads in agreement. I was so relieved I ran up to Delilah grinning because I felt good from all the attention. I liked the feeling of getting people to agree with me. I was already thinking how to create more of that feeling. Brenda thought I liked my dresses more than her pants. The voices in my head seem to get mad at my temporary moment of peace. I had to remember this feeling and remember how I got here because most days I am so numb I forget a lot of things. I was constantly trying to prepare for the next tragedy. I was creating a "trauma" that would take years to be treated.

After my victory, I wanted Delilah to be proud of me but she just rolled her eyes and sucked her teeth. I didn't care. I was just happy she did something.

As we entered the school I was already working out a plan in my head trying to figure out how to get Ms. Mallory to give me a compliment in front of Brenda so I could keep this attention streak going. The voices in my head were even jealous. I didn't care... nobody could see them and I wasn't going to introduce them to anybody because even at five I knew that would cause more problems for Delilah and me.

I need God to find my Momma and quick! The bell rings and we head to class.

THE CHRISTIAN CONVERSATION

Mrs. Hallstead smiles as she watches the girls walk to school with the other kids in the neighborhood. "The girls are finally off to school and I still can't believe I have children in my house. I wanted boys but Gawd sent me girls. Even Charles seems a little too excited so I will have to keep my eye on him. I know that looks all too well because as a child, my uncles looked at me the same way. But prayer is what I can rely on. And I will pray Gawd keeps them safe. This is my blessing, just like I was my aunt's blessings when my momma died. She didn't let nothing stop her from being a momma. I have wanted to be a mother all my life but after that car accident that took my arm, my woman hood and my parents, I never thought I could be a mother; and nothing is going to stand in my way." The phone begins to ring in the kitchen, interrupting my thoughts.

"Hello? Helloooo?" says Mrs. Hallstead. Now who is playing on this phone this morning so I repeat for the last time, "Hellloooo!"

"Yes, yes! Is this, um, Mizz Hallstead?" says a low voice, barely audible on the telephone. Now who in the devil is calling my house and doesn't know me, but I put on my Christian voice just in case it's a member from the church. "Yes it is."

"Oh, well, dis here is Mizz Freeman, the girls Big Momma."

Fear immediately grips at my heart, as I am thinking in my mind, "How did she find them? What does she want? I was not giving them back!" But I begin to speak very Christian like, "Praise the Lord! How can I help you Mizz Freeman?" Meanwhile I am thinking, "This devil is trying to steal my joy."

"The social worker gave me your information and I was calling to see how the girls were", said Big Momma.

"They are blessed, Sis Freeman", said Mrs. Hallstead, "and you can call me Sis Bessie."

Big Momma was not going to be out done so she said, "Gawd is good ain't He...and you can call me Sis Connie."

As both women silently struggled with who was being more Christian, the conversation became strained and unproductive until they both decided that it would be in the best interest of the girls that no one from the family speak to them while they were in foster care. It would just confuse them and make them sad. Two women with no high school diploma and untreated trauma, were making a decision that would impact the mental state of two girls that had become wards of the great state of Virginia.

THE CHURCH MIXER

Sunday mornings come like clockwork every six days. I don't know if I was supposed to be happy or sad. This is the only time I really see Mr. and Mrs. Hallstead talk to each other. Most of the time, Mrs. Hallstead is in the kitchen cooking or in the small living room reading the Bible. Sometimes I wonder what the Bible really be sayin' because so far it doesn't answer any of my prayers and God can't seem to locate my momma. But Mrs. Halstead says I shouldn't question God so I pretend I don't; but when I'm at the window looking at heaven, I always ask a lot of questions. I feel like I hear God speak but I forget most of what He says. I think if He allows me to remember, I could plan the escape or locate this woman called my momma.

I am beginning to think she doesn't want to be found. It does not take that long to find your kids. Everywhere we go I see kids with their Momma and Daddy. What is so bad about us that makes us unwanted? I will just work harder at being good and maybe someone can let the jail people know that my momma got kids and she needs to come home.

We in the back of the car and headed to Green Street Baptist Church. It is time to visit the candy lady and have fun talking to the other church kids. Well that's what I dream about anyway.

Delilah and I are the only kids that have to sit up front with parents. I glance at Delilah but she is staring in space as usual as if she is not even there. Sometimes I see a black cloud all around her and it's trying to cover her so I can't see her but I begin to pray to God and ask him to remove it so I can see her. Words that come to my mind at five to say, come out of nowhere. Sometimes when the voices get too loud in my head I would tell them God said, "Shut up!" and they would be quiet but then I would get lonely and start talking to them again. If Delilah would start talking out of her mouth and not with her eyes, I swear I would leave these voices alone. But the voices are nice to me sometimes, especially when I am thinking of how I can rid Mr. Hallstead from turning into the Devil at night. If I talked to God too much, they started yelling at me that my momma ain't never coming back; however, I was getting used to being disappointed. I had learned in a very short period of time, foster care and disappointments go together.

As we walk in church, I put on my 1000 watt smile. I got to make the Hallsteads look good but I promise you before the end of service, I will find a way to get me a piece of candy from one of them church kids. I will just use the persuasion I used on Brenda.

The Pastor. That's what Black folk call the man that stands on the big stage and scream and sweat for thirty minutes, then everyone gives him money, we pray and then leave.

Church must have been good today because Mrs. Hallstead said we were going to get chicken from Moses' Chicken. Now I love to eat and I didn't love anything in particular. I just liked food that was bought from a restaurant. I wish it was a McDonald's cheeseburger but if we were going to buy it that was good enough for me.

It was something about eating food that was paid for that made me feel special. I wanted to make sure I did not get in trouble before we got to the chicken place. Those voices in my head got me in trouble a few times because of my mouth. If I saw something that made me curious, I would ask a question but Mrs. Hallstead would say, "stay in a child's place." This was confusing to me because I was born grown so I had no clue what that place looked like. I had to look out for everyone because if I didn't nobody seemed to get along. I was the glue and if I didn't pretend to be happy, nobody talked to each other. The only time Mr. Hallstead talked was when he was giving orders or beating our asses. Yeah we got beatens, mostly for being curious about life. I needed answers and as much as I wanted to stay quiet, sometimes my mouth would not cooperate. But not today. I wanted that chicken and nothing was getting in my way.

SPOKEN WORDS

We are approaching six months being in this foster care system. I felt more like a frost child than a foster child. Delilah still was not talking and I was at the window everyday trying to convince God to find my momma. I guess He is not ready to do that because she is not here yet. We finally have some action in the neighborhood. A family moves in next door with some kids, three boys to be exact. Now the Hallsteads don't let us out of the house to play that often but when Mrs. Hallstead washes clothes, she hangs them on the clothes line in the backyard. Since we share the same backyard as our neighbors, we can see who is outside playing.

I didn't know much about boys at five years old but they seemed weird 'cause they were always staring at Delilah. I would catch her looking at one in particular; he must have been the oldest cause he bossed the other two around. They had a dog and one day when we were outside in the yard playing, the boys came out with their dog. Now I don't like anything walking on four legs. I am already dealing with these voices and mute Delilah and now a dog! No thank you.

But on this particular day, the oldest was determined to get Delilah's attention so he let go of his dog; and wouldn't you know it, it ran straight toward me and Delilah! Now I took off but Delilah was too slow and the dog caught up with her. For the first time in six months she screamed at the top of her voice, "MOMMA!" And that dog must have got spooked cause it took off toward that oldest boy! I laughed so hard I almost forgot she was talking.

Mrs. Hallstead came out of the house and looked at her and said, "Stop all that yelling!" I just looked at Delilah and she looked at me and we both bust out laughing. I was laughing because now I had my sister and I guess for just a moment, she allowed herself to just enjoy the moment of having fun.

The boys got the biggest eye roll from me but I think my sister smiled at the oldest boy. Mmmm...weird but she was talking to me and that made me happy if just for a moment .

LYNORA

[Meanwhile in Goochland, Va.]

The last time I attempted to think, all I could do was scream in my head and be mad at Big Momma. So let me introduce myself again. My name is Lynora but I go by Greta. I'm nineteen years old with two girls that live in foster care. I guess you can say I was a foster kid too. My mother died when I was eight years old from an asthma attack. My father could not take care of all five of us so some family members thought it would be a good idea to split us up based on our complexion. The darker kids stayed in the South, the lighter kids went up North. I was brown with "pretty hair" so I was able to go to Virginia with Big Momma. I learned real quick all family ain't good family. They didn't treat me like we had the same last name and they made sure I knew I was just a paycheck.

But that's not going to be the case with my girls. Since I woke up in jail almost four years ago, I have been trying to find my girls. It took me sleeping with one of the guards but I heard they are with the Hallsteads. The social worker told me they are some good Christian people and when I get out of lock up, I'm going to get my girls. But today is going to be a good day. Being in this good prison system they allow your kids to come visit you on family day once a month. They are bringing my babies to see me for family day! Delilah is my oldest and my favorite. When I was pregnant with her I thought, "Finally I'll have something that will love me," and when she popped out, I fell in love for the first time. I told plenty of men I loved them over the years but all I was just trying to do was get what was in their wallets. Being pretty got you a pocket full of money from men. Now when I had my second baby, I swear she came out talking. I heard she is always asking people all these questions about why I leave her. I keep trying to explain to her in the letters I write from jail that I didn't leave them. One day I came home from one of my binges and Big Momma told me "the people" came and got them. I lost it. I started drinking more and getting high, I didn't speak for months. I did some petty crimes and it landed me here in jail. I didn't know how to fight for my girls because nobody fought for me. Sometimes I just wanted to forget the pain I felt; that's why I got high and stayed drunk all the time. I felt like I was always invisible until men started showing me attention. I welcomed it and two babies later, I'm locked up and have no idea who the daddies are.

"Lynora!" screamed my cellie. "They're here!"

Yeah, today gonna be a good day. My babies' here!

THE CONJUGAL VISIT

It's been about four years and I am nine and Delilah is ten. We are only eleven months apart so for almost thirty days each year, we are the same age.

Now that Delilah is talking I have a somewhat of a talking partner. We still mostly talk with our eyes or sometimes I swear I can hear her speak in my head. I guess that's what people call telepathy. Since we have been here, we have been introduced to the Lord and Monday night prayer meeting, but still no McDonald's on a regular... and we don't ever go outside to play with other kids; especially after Delilah got chased by the neighbor's dog.

No one mentions the events that happen when the sun goes down or the fact that we haven't had an ounce of counseling. We've seen three Christmases and we get three used items from social service. Now where the other money goes I am not sure but if I hear one more time, "If you don't act right, I'm going to call the people to come get you," I'm going to call them myself but then I remember, no disrespect and I quickly adjust my mask and 1000 watt smile.

Now today we are supposed to be in school but we are going to see our real Momma in jail. Yeah... jail! Even at nine I knew that's not normal because no one else I go to school with has ever mentioned visits to jail to see their parents. But in the foster care system, in the 80's, you just do what they tell you. So we are off to see our real momma in jail.

BLURRED LINES

I'm lying in bed and it's almost time to get up for school. I can't sleep. All I can think about is Greta, my biological mother. Her first name is Lynora but I call her by her middle name because all her prison friends called her that. She couldn't stop showing us off today. Everyone we walked past she told them, "These are my girls!" The entire time I was thinking, "How come you are not taking care of us? How come we got to call some other folk Momma and Daddy?" Instead of screaming my thoughts at the top of my lungs, I just walk around and put on that 1000 watt smile I have learned to master so well. Plus, I need to do this for her because this nine year old wants her to be proud of her and love her back; and maybe just maybe, all those sessions in the window will pay off and she will come and get us so the sun can set and the Devil will not come for Delilah. But for now I will just smile.

"Ariel!" said Delilah.

"What?"

"Are you sleeping?"

"No," I said. "Why?"

"Well you better go to sleep. We have school tomorrow!"

We both sigh and sleep finds me instantly. Morning comes too fast and we are running around trying to get ready. We don't have much of a selection of clothes so getting dressed takes less than five minutes. That's the easy part of the morning. The house is as big as a matchbox with one bathroom and two very small bedrooms. If it wasn't for the kitchen and living room it would be considered a studio apartment. We walk to school so it's not like we have a bus to catch. We finish getting dressed and head out the door.

We have been living in Douglass Park for about eight years now and since we can't go outside and play (except in the backyard) we never get an opportunity to socialize with the other kids. So going to school is more for my social outlet than learning. I swear with all these thoughts running through my head I can barely concentrate on any school work.

Delilah is the complete opposite of me. She is smarter than Einstein and Sigmund and Freud put together. She can read or hear something once and she knows it for life. I guess that's why she always comes home with straight A's on her report card. I can barely manage to get a high B but I guess if I could control my thoughts, I could hear what the teachers are saying.

I really don't remember any events from elementary to middle school except the big snowstorm of the 80's, and when I got my appendix taken out at the age of ten. Blocking out events had become my coping mechanism. My brain had learned to survive in overload. I guess you could say that I operated on ten every waking minute of the day. I don't recall ever having a day of rest with my thoughts and if it was a relief, I was in a conscious state of black out so my memory has been functioning dysfunctionally since the age of five. I can only describe it as being disconnected from your power source for a lifetime. I was truly a case of the walking dead. Of all the events of my childhood that were blocked out, I do remember one family in the neighborhood called the Roses, and no they did not look, smell, or act like those flowers. The entire family would be considered bullies today and they were never seen without three or four of them together.

The best way to describe them was an army of soldiers that were dedicated to protecting anything that tried to divide them. Most of the houses on Carter Circle (in Douglass Park where we used to live) were row houses, with three or four houses attached. I swear one set of rowhomes alone housed all of them! On the rare occasions when we were allowed outside in the front yard, I can still remember the Roses going into each other houses while babies in diapers were running around outside from the door being left open or from anyone who entered or exited the house. One thing I did envy about them was that they all looked alike and they had this bond that was unfamiliar to me. If they didn't want to smile they didn't. No one seemed to mind if you said "no" or if you didn't want to do something, and the children called the adults, momma and daddy, aunties and uncles; titles that only existed in my imagination.

I was yearning for a bond with relatives...any connection to a pulse. I needed to get myself off of life support. At the age of fourteen I didn't know that what I was describing was an unconditional bond that I yearned for daily and it was called family. It was something I knew I didn't have so I just pretended that my life was different. Everyone I met I would mentally take on their life and pretend it was mine. I guess you could say I became a lot of people which led me to have the ability to adapt and become whoever I needed to be for the moment. It worked most of the time and I did it so well. I became the original creator of "fake it til' you make it" phrase. By the time I was fourteen and and in the tenth grade, I had mastered that 1000 watt smile, and my multiple personalities had become my immediate family.

I attended the tenth grade at a high school in P town, which was in Va. The P stood for Portsmouth and the high school was not far from Daniel Park but we had to take the school bus which was exciting because outings were non-existent unless it was going to church or prayer meeting. Thus, my social skills developed courtesy of the public school system. The school was mostly a mixture of black and white students but since I got along with everyone, color was never my concern at the time. I was fascinated with the fact that most of the kids had their real parents raising them. Their parents were young and I was fascinated by the resemblance of a child to the parent. I would try to imagine what Greta would look like if I saw her. I would go into the bathroom in school and look through the blurry mirrors and pretend she was coming to pick me up today. I wished for the day I could yell

"Momma", just one time and it be my truth. We had long stopped going to visit Greta in jail and whatever I did remember about her had turned into a blur. I think I became very disappointed in God but I didn't want Him to be mad at me so I kept it to myself. But when I went to the window now, my faith was almost non-existent. The sun did not shine as brightly as it used to when I was five. I talked to God out of habit more than anything and sometimes I would just sit in the window just to look out of it and see what was on the other side, still planning my escape.

Delilah had transferred to a school where you had to have good grades to attend so even though we still lived in the same house and in the same room, we became distant and invisible to our own surroundings. I knew I needed to find a connection to something and I didn't care if it was safe, boring or dangerous. Anything with a pulse would be okay with me because sometimes I swear I couldn't feel mine. As I had gotten older I began to understand just how alone I was and the need to belong became so unbearable that sometimes I would talk to myself. So when I saw Valencia Banks walking down the hall of Carter High School with her group of girlfriends, I knew I wanted in. Valencia always wore the latest designer clothes and her group always seemed to be having so much fun. They would have conversations about their cousins and siblings and parents, and I remember wanting to fit in so badly. I started my own version of the Daniel family tree. That was my real last name and that was the only truth in the stories I told. So I began my version of my family tree. I had more aunties and uncles I knew what to do with and in my mind I was the happiest kid in the world. My reality started intertwining with my lies so much I started believing them. I just wanted to experience one minute of normal to see what it felt like to know someone who had the same blood as mine running through their veins. Nobody ever called the Hallsteads house. I don't ever remember hearing the phone ring or anyone ever asking to speak to me or Delilah to just check on us. Neglect comes in many forms and I really understand how people can die from a broken heart because I died a thousand deaths in foster care, but for now Valencia and her crew became the audience to my lies and that would just have to be how I built the Daniel family tree until Greta came to her senses.

High school exposes you to everything and 1985 was all about double belts and skinny leg pants. All the popular kids were dressed in the latest fashion from head to toe but I already knew if it didn't come with the three items from social service that we got for Christmas, I was not getting it. So I did the next best thing. I took two safety pins and pinned my pants at the bottom. Mrs. Hallstead finally let me wear pants that she bought from the thrift store but I was just happy to finally look somewhat like the other kids.

"Hey Girl!" exclaimed Valencia. I turned around to see her standing near the locker I was leaning against to fix my pants.

"Hey Girl!" I said, trying to sound just as unbothered as her. Meanwhile I am thinking "Does my pants look as fake as my smile?"

As I came back into focus I heard her saying, "You ready to head to English?" and with my 1000 watt smile I said, "Yep!" English has always been my favorite subject. It allowed me the opportunity to make words come to life. I was a great storyteller and I knew one day I was going to write and everyone was going to love every word of it. But for now, I just hoped one day I would get a pair of real skinny leg pants. Meanwhile, me and my safety pins followed behind Valencia to English class with all my personalities in tow.

Volume 14

PSYCHOLOGICALLY FROZEN

It's a Saturday morning and I am reflecting on my life. It has had some drastic changes over the last two years. I am at my usual spot sitting at the window trying to have a conversation with God. The question is still the same as it has been for the last eleven years, "Why can't Greta come find us?" I am sixteen and a lot has changed. I heard my Big Momma died and my Aunt Wanda Faye. I don't know how to feel because I haven't seen them since we left Big Momma's house. Delilah is no longer living in the house with me. She had a baby and had to leave the house but I think the baby saved her from the Devil coming to get her when the sun went down. I am just as confused now as when I was five and arrived at the Hallstead's house. My only outlet is school and I think I can recall maybe once being allowed to go to the mall and that was with Valencia. Insanity was my best friend and I was clueless to what my reality was. I started to resent God.

By the time my senior year arrived, I had lost my virginity to the neighborhood boy. I still was not among the best dressed even though I had a job at my favorite spot, Mcdonald's. Now I could have as many cheeseburgers as I wanted. Sometimes I would help Delilah with my nephew Kirk. His daddy went to the same church we attended. I don't remember much about Kirk's daddy. I guess I must have dozed off on that portion of the service because the next thing I remember was seeing Delilah with a big belly and then hearing her screaming at the top of her lungs, "It hurt! It hurt!" Soon the baby was in her arms and then she was gone. I never had a chance to talk to her about her relationship or any relationship with boys for that matter.

To always feel invisible your entire life and then one day start getting attention from a popular boy in the neighborhood made me believe that I was in love. So the fall of my junior year I would look forward to the bus rides to school because that's when Alan would talk to me. I felt something for the first time that felt warm and finally connected me to a pulse. I had no clue of how to date a boy, be a girl or not get pregnant. My foster mother said one thing..."Keep your legs closed and your dress down." So when Alan started showing me attention I did what any naive sixteen year old with loud thoughts in her head would do... I fell hard and fast, and before I knew it, I was skipping school and yearning for that attention that gave me a pulse every time I was around him. Lack is a powerful drug and it had me strung out waiting for the next hit. Needless to say I loved the feeling I had with Alan. I was never taught how not to get pregnant so I did the exact opposite of what my foster mom said. It wasn't to long after me and Alan started having sex that I discovered I was pregnant.

I didn't want to disappear like my sister so I found a way out. I heard a group of girls in school talking about a place that took care of the problem. My reality at home was not the greatest but it was my normal, and although it was traumatic in so many ways the thought of disappearing like Delilah terrified me. So I had an abortion. I should have gotten rid of the boy instead! The day I went to get the abortion, I sat in that car with Alan for about two hours trying to figure out how to keep this life growing in me without disappearing from the Hallsteads house. Nothing came to mind so I took care of the problem. Looking back on that journey of becoming a woman, I realize how important relationships are and how much time I wasted trying to deny my sister's existence because of the pain it caused me. I realized trying to feel anything outside the bubble I had created to protect my sanity without counseling is when I fell into the same situation as my sister. I thought getting rid of the problem would get rid of the memory too.

I believed that Greta had done the same thing with us. She had two babies and forgot to raise us. So instead of having a baby that would have loud thoughts and have to make up lies

about a family tree, I would take it out of its misery.

ONE MINUTE TO LOVE

I used my body as payment until the supplier no longer wanted to sample my goods and services. I was once again going through an emotional withdrawal until the next supplier came along. In the meantime, I would try to kick the habit of a loveless life by blaming my crackhead mother of all my pain but we were both junkies....her to a substance and me to an emotion. I would cry for hours trying to understand the will of God. As I sat in that window waiting for God to give me an answer that would give me peace for just one minute to feel love but silence was all that met my thoughts. Soon another supplier would come along and extinguish the blaze but the brimstone would be forever burning, eating away at my sanity. It took my flesh to places I almost didn't survive. The guilt and shame I felt was something else I had to add to my already crowded mind. One day I was so overloaded I thought about suicide for a brief moment but the need for me to people please saved my life.

After the abortion, I stopped having sex. Alan moved on to another conquest and I was left with all my different personalities and an even bigger hole in my heart. Since I didn't want to risk getting pregnant again (especially since I'm still not sure how it happened in the first place), I kept my dress down and I kept my legs closed.

When senior year had finally arrived, I had all but given up on Greta. I was hardly in the window asking God for anything anymore. I felt like I had to take matters into my own hands. I knew that after all these years of planning my escape, the time had come to put the plan into motion. I would join the military! Recruiters were always at the high school and they must have seen the desperation in my face. I decided to enlist in the Army because they asked first. Even though I had no idea what a march was or what being a soldier would mean, I knew I could finally get out of the

Hallstead's house and find my own identity. Social Service would be a thing of the past and they could keep those three crappy gifts at Christmas! Me and my personalities were outta here.

"Ariel?"

"Yes Momma!"

"You sure you want to go in the Army?"

I looked at Mrs. Hallstead and almost said "No" because I saw this look of loneliness that I had never really recognized before. I finally took a good look at Mrs. Hallstead and realized that she was a victim of her circumstance just like me and at that moment I wanted to save her but I had to save me first. So I said, "Yes, I am sure."

ON TO THE NEXT

The night I graduated from high school was just like any other big occasion for me. No fuss over me; no aunties or uncles to come and congratulate me, or make a big fuss. Just the Hallsteads and me. Delilah didn't even come to my graduation. We had stopped all communication by my senior year of high school. Foster care had taught me early on how to distance myself from any emotions that caused me pain and that tomorrow would be a new day. I would be a high school graduate, and in two months, me and all my personalities would be on our way to becoming a soldier in the US Army. Little did I know this journey was setting me up for my next set of lessons in life, becoming the

"Other Woman's Voice"...

"Ariel Daniels, please raise your right hand..."

THE END

*****

Alice P. Davis, who writes under the pen name *Jay G Davis* was raised in the foster care system until the age of 18.

Davis is a Veteran of the United States Army. She is the mother of one daughter. Davis enjoys her career as a flight attendant and traveling all over the world. Davis has used her experiences to be the blueprint to introduce her characters and life experiences to the literary world.

www.ingramcontent.com/pod-product-compliance
Lightning Source LLC
Chambersburg PA
CBHW071413170626
46811CB00003B/1387